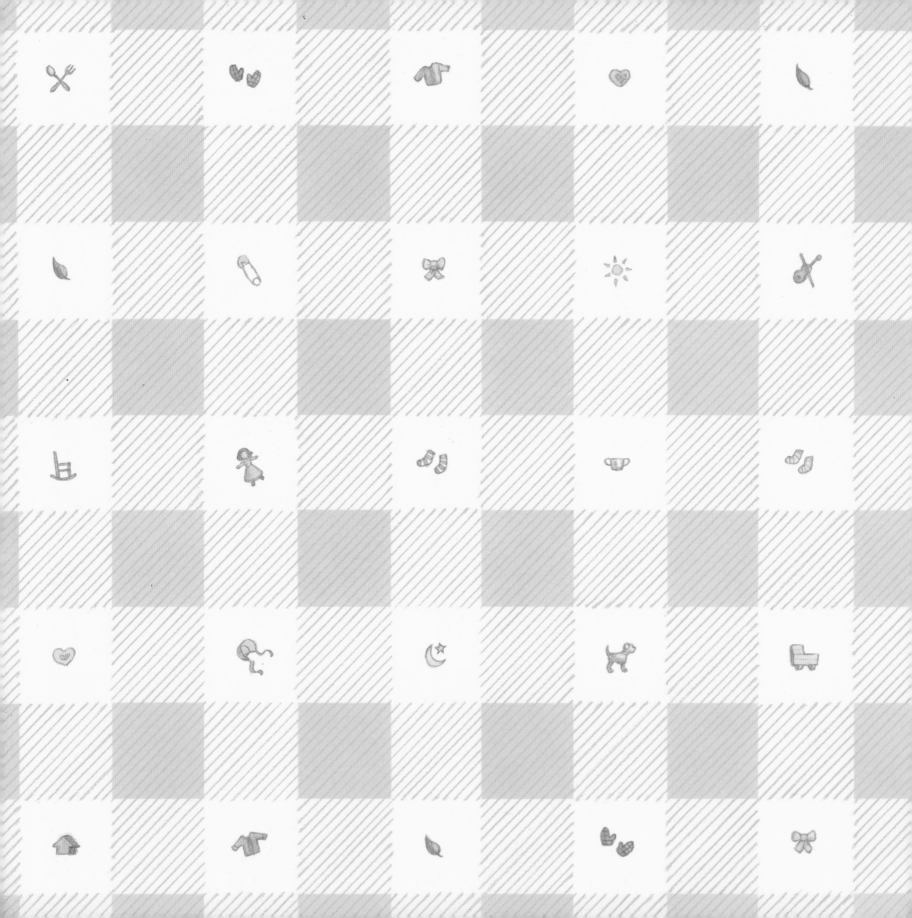

The
Little House
Baby Book

For
David Holly
R.G.

The Little House Baby Book

BASED ON THE LITTLE HOUSE BOOKS BY

LAURA INGALLS WILDER

DESIGNED AND ILLUSTRATED BY

RENÉE GRAEF

HarperFestival®
A Division of HarperCollinsPublishers

Also designed and illustrated by Reneé Graef:

The Little House Baby Photograph Album
The perfect place to save baby's pictures

This Book Belongs To:

My Name

My name was chosen by _____

I was given my name because _____

My name means _____

Pet names or nicknames _____

Other names my parents considered _____

If I had been a _____ , my parents would have called me _____

*Pa would throw off his fur cap
and coat and mittens, and call:
"Where's my little half-pint of sweet cider
half drunk up?" That was Laura,
because she was so small.*
—LITTLE HOUSE IN THE BIG WOODS

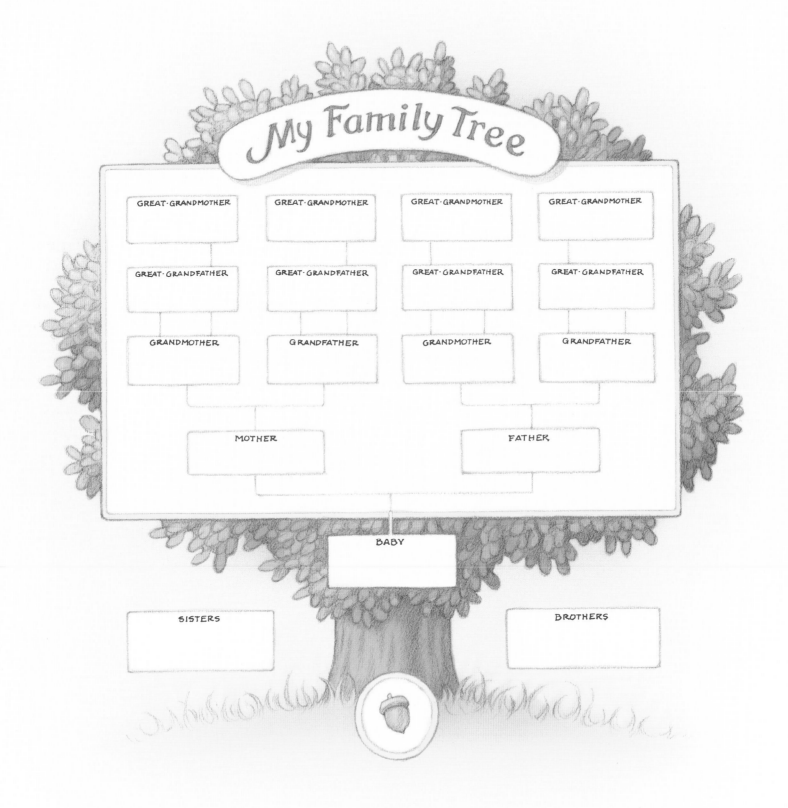

My Family Tree

| GREAT·GRANDMOTHER | GREAT·GRANDMOTHER | GREAT·GRANDMOTHER | GREAT·GRANDMOTHER |

| GREAT·GRANDFATHER | GREAT·GRANDFATHER | GREAT·GRANDFATHER | GREAT·GRANDFATHER |

| GRANDMOTHER | GRANDFATHER | GRANDMOTHER | GRANDFATHER |

MOTHER

FATHER

BABY

SISTERS

BROTHERS

I'm Born!

My name is

_____

I was born on _____ at _____

On a

_____

In

_____

I was delivered by

_____

When My Parents First Saw Me

My Mother said _____

_____

_____

_____

_____

_____

_____

My Father said _____

_____

_____

_____

_____

My Birth Announcement
or Birth Certificate

My Parents

What I Looked Like

The color of my
hair was _____

The color of my
eyes was _____

My weight was

My height was

I had these iden-
tifying marks _____

I resembled _____

Date _____

My First Picture

Taken by _____

Taken at _____

The World When I Was Born

The President of the United States was _____

The Vice President of the United States was _____

Headlines the day I was born _____

_____

_____

The weather the day I was born _____

Current events _____

_____

_____

New inventions _____

_____

Trends and Fads _____

_____

_____

_____

The most popular television show was _____

_____

The most popular song was _____

The movie which won the Academy Award was _____

_____

There had never been such wonders
in the whole history of the world, Pa said.
Now in one morning they had actually traveled
a whole week's journey, and Laura had seen
the Iron Horse turn around, to go back the
whole way in one afternoon.
— BY THE SHORES OF SILVER LAKE

My First Visitors

...And What They Said

Some Gifts   I Received

Gifts   From

Gifts   From

Where I Lived

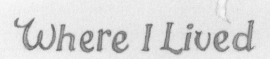

Address of my first home

_____

Later addresses	When I moved

_Laura went under those singing
flowers into the dugout. It was one room,
all white. The earth walls had been
smoothed and white-washed. The earth floor
was smooth and hard._

~ON THE BANKS OF PLUM CREEK

Teething

My first tooth appeared _____

_____

_____

_____

_____

_____   _____

_____   BABY'S   _____
TEETH
_____   _____

My First Visits to the Doctor

My pediatrician's name was

_____

My pediatrician's address and phone number were

_____

Date	Why I went	What my pediatrician said

*Laura swallowed a bitter swallow
and tried to turn her head away, but the cup
followed her mouth. The mellow, deep voice
said again, "Drink it. It will make you well."
So Laura swallowed the whole bitter dose.*

—LITTLE HOUSE ON THE PRAIRIE

My Immunization Record

My blood type _____

Type of vaccine	1ST DOSE	2nd DOSE	3rd DOSE	4th DOSE
DPT				
Polio				
MMR				
HIB				

My First Month

A Typical day

6 a.m. _____
7 a.m. _____
8 a.m. _____
9 a.m. _____
10 a.m. _____
11 a.m. _____
NOON _____
1 p.m. _____
2 p.m. _____
3 p.m. _____
4 p.m. _____
5 p.m. _____
6 p.m. _____
7 p.m. _____
8 p.m. _____
9 p.m. _____
10 p.m. _____
11 p.m. _____
MID-NIGHT _____
1 a.m. _____
2 a.m. _____
3 a.m. _____
4 a.m. _____
5 a.m. _____

I Began to Grow

MONTH	HEIGHT INCHES	WEIGHT POUNDS
FIRST		
SECOND		
THIRD		
FOURTH		
FIFTH		
SIXTH		
SEVENTH		
EIGHTH		
NINTH		
TENTH		
ELEVENTH		
TWELFTH		

"Ouch! My toes are tight!" Laura exclaimed.
"I should say they are," Pa said.
"Your feet have grown since last winter."
—ON THE BANKS OF PLUM CREEK

My Journeys and Outings

My first trip outdoors was on _____

We went to _____

I wore _____

This is how I reacted _____

I went most often to _____

My longest trip was to _____

_____

In the mornings they ran through
the dewy chill grass that wet their feet
and dabbled the hem of their dresses. They liked to
splash their bare feet through the grass all
strung with dewdrops. They liked to watch the sun
rise over the edge of the world.
—ON THE BANKS OF PLUM CREEK

My Favorite Places to Visit

_____

_____

_____

_____

_____

_____

_____

_____

_____

Laura loved Grandma's house.

— LITTLE HOUSE IN THE BIG WOODS

My Favorite Things

Toys _____

_____

_____ Games _____

_____ Stories _____

_____ Music _____

_____ Clothes _____

_____

Other _____

One game they loved to play
was called mad dog. Pa would run his fingers
through his thick, brown hair, standing it all on
end. Then he dropped on all fours and,
growling, he chased Laura and Mary around
the room, trying to get them cornered
where they couldn't get away.
— LITTLE HOUSE IN THE BIG WOODS

My First Haircut

My first lock of hair

Where I got my hair cut

_____

_____

Date

_____

I first lifted my head _____

_____

I recognized familiar faces _____

_____

First bath _____

I held my head steady _____

My first nail trim _____

I first rolled over _____

I turned on my side _____

My first smile _____

I slept through the night _____

Laura took a hold of the pony's mane.
But the pony was much larger than she was,
its back was high, and the pony was strong.
Laura said, "I don't know if I can. I
never did ride horseback."
~ BY THE SHORES OF SILVER LAKE

Memorable Firsts

I played peekaboo

I first said "dada"

I first said "mama"

My first laugh

I first clapped

I first crawled

Laura and Mary had never been
to a party and did not quite know what it would
be like. Ma said it was a pleasant time
friends had together.
—ON THE BANKS OF PLUM CREEK

I first waved ....

Other memorables ....

_____

_____

_____

_____

_____

_____

_____

The Way I Ate

The first time I drank
from a bottle _____

_____

The first time I held a spoon
_____

The first time I drank from
a cup _____

_____

The first time I ate at the
table, I behaved like this
_____

_____

☆ ☆ ☆ ☆ ☆ ☆ ☆ ☆ ☆ ☆

My favorite foods _____

_____

_____

_____

_____

My "unfavorite" foods _____

_____

_____

_____

☆ ☆ ☆ ☆ ☆ ☆ ☆ ☆ ☆ ☆

*These new tin cups were their very own.
Now they each had a cup to drink out of.
Laura jumped up and down and shouted and laughed,
but Mary stood still and looked with shining eyes
at her own tin cup.*
—LITTLE HOUSE ON THE PRAIRIE

The Way I Slept

The first time I slept through the night _____

_____

I changed my morning nap schedule _____

_____

Did I like going to sleep? _____

_____

Favorite bedtime stories _____

_____

Favorite bedtime lullabies _____

_____

My First Steps

I first stood up with help

I first stood up alone

I first walked with help

I first walked alone

Laura looked back, and Pa waved to her.
When she stopped running she could hear the sound
of the wind in the grasses and the lippety-lapping of
the lake water. She hoppity-skipped on
the short dry grass along the shore.

—BY THE SHORES OF SILVER LAKE

My First Words

My first sounds _____

_____

_____

_____

My first phrases _____

_____

_____

_____

My first words _____

_____

_____

_____

Favorite words _____

_____

_____

_____

The People Who Took Care of Me

At the beginning

_____

_____

As I got bigger

_____

_____

_____

_____

These people helped

_____

_____

_____

_____

The name of my first babysitter was

_____

_____

This is how I reacted to my first babysitter

_____

_____

My Family and Me

It was all so pleasant, the doors
and windows wide open to the summer evening,
the dishes making little cheerful sounds
together as Ma washed them and Mary and
Laura wiped, and Pa putting away
the fiddle and smiling and whistling
softly to himself.
—LITTLE HOUSE IN THE BIG WOODS

Early Holidays
or Religious Ceremonies

My First  Birthday

Where I celebrated my
birthday _____

_____

These were my guests

_____

_____

_____

_____

The games we played

_____

_____

This is what we ate

_____

_____

This is how I behaved

_____

I received these gifts

_____

_____

_____

_____

This is what the weather
was like _____

_____

That night, for a special birthday treat,
Pa played "Pop! Goes the Weasel" for Laura.
—LITTLE HOUSE IN THE BIG WOODS

My First Birthday

My Schedule at One Year

In the morning _____

In the evening _____

In the afternoon _____

At night _____

Each day had its own proper work. Ma used to say,
"Wash on Monday,
Iron on Tuesday,
Mend on Wednesday,
Churn on Thursday,
Clean on Friday,
Bake on Saturday,
Rest on Sunday."
—LITTLE HOUSE IN THE BIG WOODS

My Personality at One Year

*The large bright stars hung down
from the sky. Lower and lower they came, quivering
with music. Laura gasped, and Ma came quickly.
"What is it, Laura?" she asked, and Laura whispered,
"The stars are singing."*
—LITTLE HOUSE ON THE PRAIRIE

Two...Three

My Mischiefs

"Laura!" Mary cried. "Pa said we mustn't!"
Laura was climbing. "He did not, either!" she
contradicted. "He did not say we must not climb up it.
He said we must not slide down it.
I'm only climbing."
—ON THE BANKS OF PLUM CREEK

Funny Things I Did and Said

Favorite Outfit

XXX

New Journeys and Experiences

*Laura would rather not stop anywhere.
She would rather go on and on, to the very end
of the road, wherever it was.*
—BY THE SHORES OF SILVER LAKE

Three...Four

My First Day at School

_The teacher said to Laura and Carrie,
"You're new, aren't you?" She was a smiling young
lady, with curled bangs. The bodice of her black
dress was buttoned down the front
with twinkling jet buttons._
—THE LONG WINTER

School Days

Every day Laura liked school more.
−THE LONG WINTER

Some Happy Moments

Some Happy Moments

Some Thoughts About Me From Mother

_____

_____

_____

_____

_____

_____

_____

_____

Some Thoughts About Me From Father

Favorites at Five

Some Things I Did Best

Some Things I Did Worst

Me
and My
Friends

Me
and My
Friends

Just Me

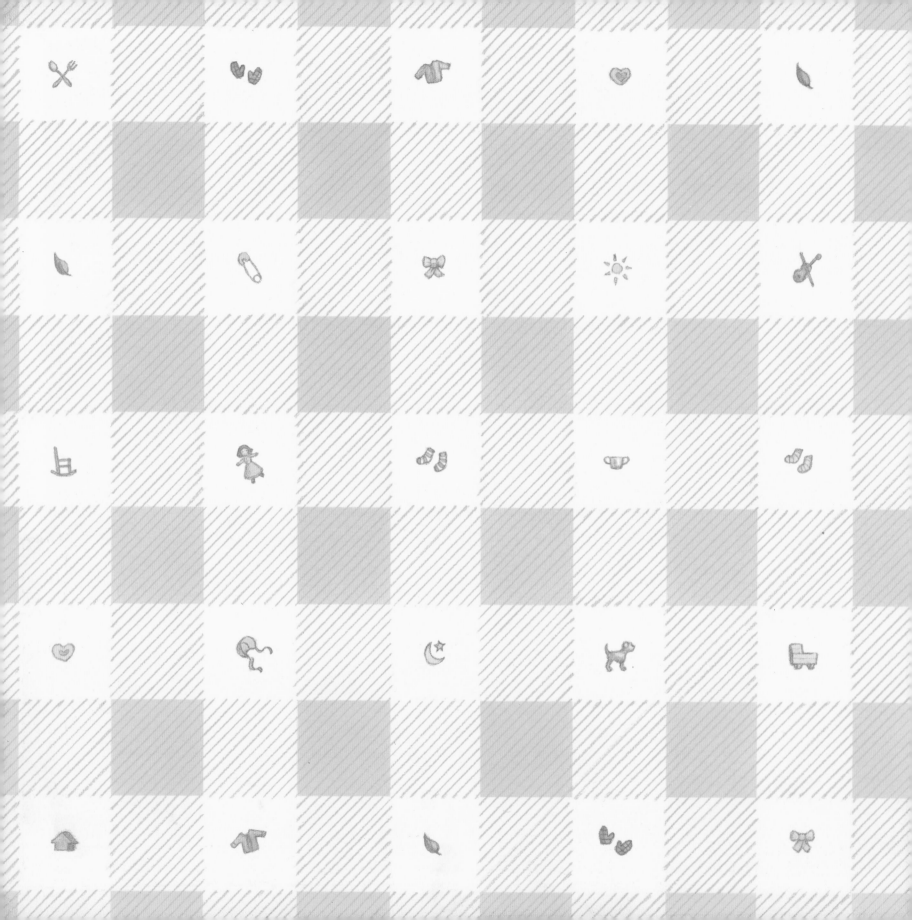